THE
MAGNIFICENT
BOOK OF TREASURES
ANCIENT
GREECE

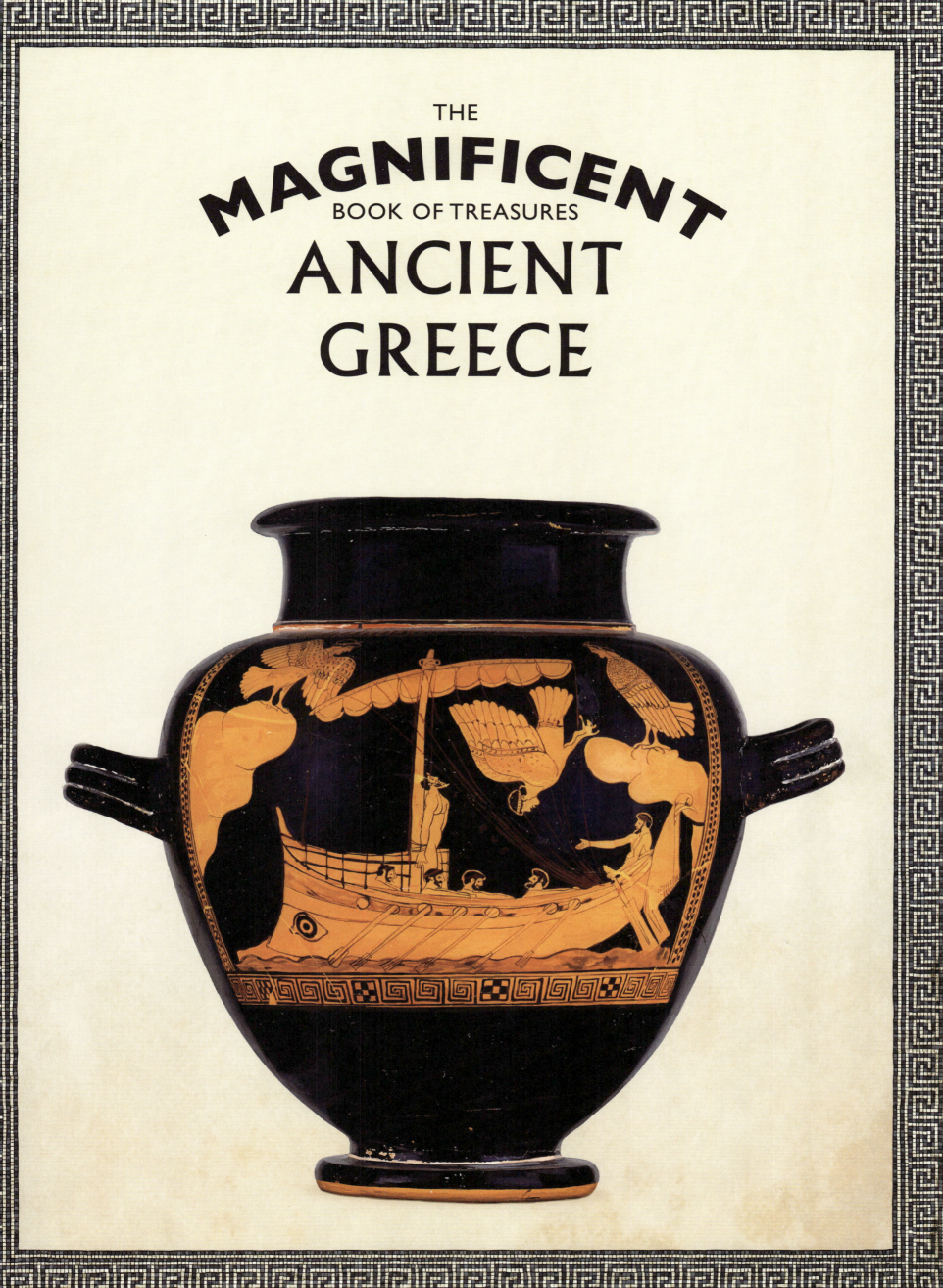

THE MAGNIFICENT BOOK OF TREASURES
ANCIENT GREECE

ILLUSTRATED BY EUGENIA NOBATI,
LISA ALDERSON, AND DANIEL RODGERS
WRITTEN BY GEORGE MAUDSLEY

Written by George Maudsley
Illustrated by Eugenia Nobati, Lisa Alderson, and Daniel Rodgers
Consultant: Dr. Philip Matyszak, University of Cambridge

weldonowen

Published by Weldon Owen Children's Books
An imprint of Weldon Owen International, L.P.
A subsidiary of Insight International, L.P.
PO Box 3088
San Rafael, CA 94912
www.insighteditions.com

Weldon Owen Children's Books
Senior Designer: Emma Randall
Senior Editor: Pauline Savage
Editor: Eliza Kirby
Managing Editor: Mary Beth Garhart

Insight Editions
CEO: Raoul Goff
Senior Production Manager: Greg Steffen

ISBN: 979-8-88674-067-7

Manufactured in China
First printing, May 2025. RRD0525
10 9 8 7 6 5 4 3 2 1

Insight Editions, in association with Roots of Peace, will plant
two trees for each tree used in the manufacturing of this book.

INTRODUCTION

More than 2,000 years ago, the eastern Mediterranean was alive with new ideas and discoveries and great tales of gods and goddesses. They came from a small, rocky corner of Europe—Greece. Ancient Greek culture traveled far and wide, and its influence is still felt today. Many grand buildings look like Greek temples, and modern math and science rely on Greek knowledge. We copied the ancient Greeks' greatest sporting occasion, the Olympic Games. Even their myths and legends are still retold in modern literature and films.

The Magnificent Book of Treasures: Ancient Greece takes you on a journey across this ancient world to explore its astonishing riches. See a carved athlete as he prepares to hurl a discus. Wonder at an ancient computer that revealed the paths of the planets. Meet the monstrous Medusa, and feel the winds blow as the goddess Nike descends from the sky in a storm.

Find out through a child's doll and a cup in the shape of an eagle how ordinary Greeks lived. Learn about the mighty conqueror Alexander the Great as you gaze at his face on a shining silver coin. Marvel at a king's golden death mask and a powerful warrior's armor. Discover the exploits of ancient Greek gods and heroes by studying beautiful vases, bowls, and statues.

Embark on a journey into the past to encounter some of the most magnificent ancient Greek treasures ever found.

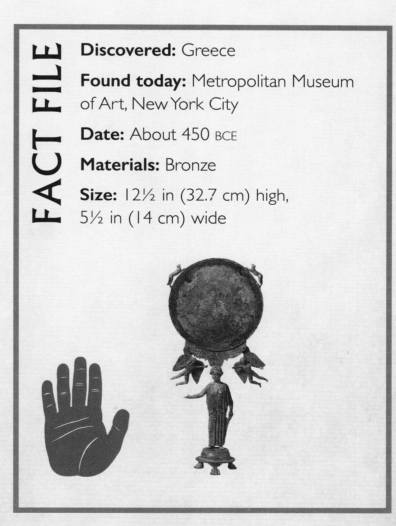

FACT FILE

Discovered: Greece

Found today: Metropolitan Museum of Art, New York City

Date: About 450 BCE

Materials: Bronze

Size: 12½ in (32.7 cm) high, 5½ in (14 cm) wide

☙ CONTENTS ☙

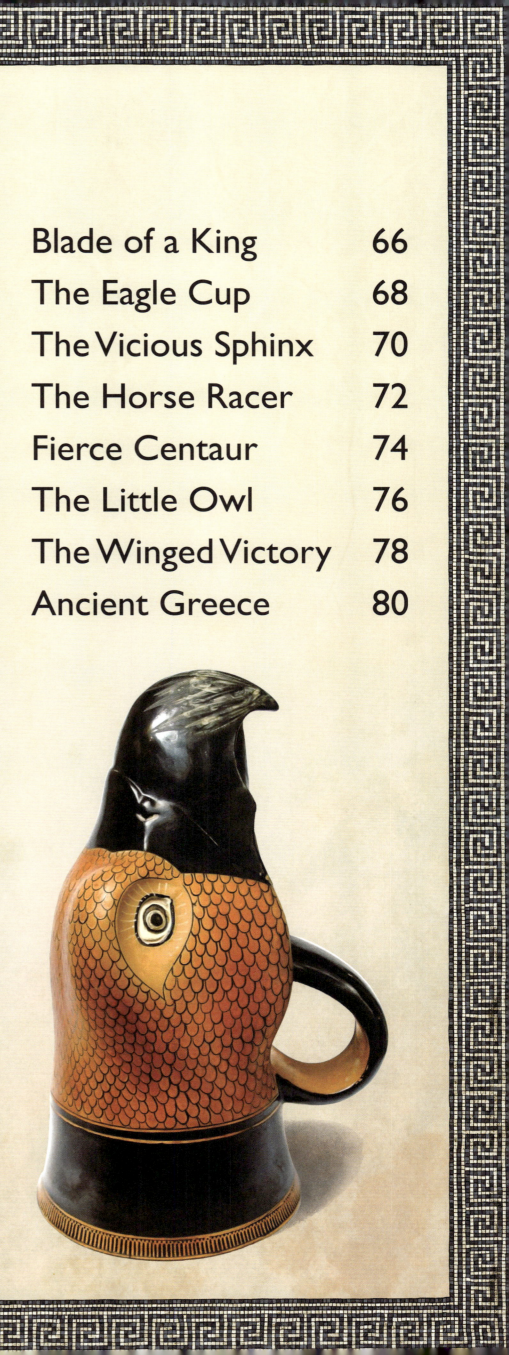

WARRIOR'S HELMET

- This gleaming bronze helmet once belonged to a hoplite, or Greek foot soldier. You can imagine the hoplite wearing it, standing shoulder to shoulder with other warriors to fight an advancing enemy.

- Hoplites were citizens of ancient Greek *poleis*, or city-states. They were mostly prosperous farmers and craftspeople who could afford armor.

- This helmet was found in a tomb. Alongside it were a spear tip and pair of bronze greaves, or shin coverings. The name of the hoplite, Denda, is engraved on one of the greaves.

- A hoplite's full suit of armor was called a panoply. As well as a helmet, it included greaves, a breastplate, shield, sword, and spear.

- This helmet was made in the Corinthian style, named after the city-state of Corinth. This design has oval-shaped eye holes, pointed cheek guards, a slit for the mouth, thin nose guard, and curved base to protect the back of the neck. It may have been topped with a crest of horsehair.

- Hoplites fought in a formation called a phalanx. The soldiers stood closely together in a rectangular shape to create a wall of shields. The hoplites pointed long weapons such as spears and pikes over the shield wall as the phalanx marched forward as a single unit.

FACT FILE

Discovered: Southern Italy

Found today: State Collection of Antiquities, Munich, Germany

Date: 500–490 BCE

Materials: Bronze

Size: About 11 in (28 cm) high

9

WILD BOAR HUNT

Amid a flurry of paws, three hounds hunt a wild boar across marshy ground in this wall painting. A dog catches the boar and sinks its teeth into the fleeing beast. On the left-hand side, the hand of a huntsman drives a spear into the boar.

This fresco, or wall painting, was once part of a larger hunting scene. The whole painting ran in a narrow strip around the walls of a room in the ancient palace of Tiryns in Greece.

The city of Tiryns was one of the centers of the ancient Mycenaean culture, Greece's first advanced civilization. It flourished for a few centuries more than three thousand years ago and gave rise to many of the myths that Greeks later enjoyed. Tiryns is also thought to be the birthplace of the hero Heracles.

Frescoes were created by painting onto fresh, wet plaster. The artist had to work quickly before the plaster dried.

Only some parts of the frescoes at Tiryns have survived. A restorer has painted in the gaps to allow us to see what the original scene was like.

FACT FILE

Discovered: Tiryns, Greece

Found today: National Archaeological Museum, Athens, Greece

Date: 1300–1200 BCE

Materials: Plaster, paint

Size: About 20 in (50 cm) high, including a decorative border

Hunting was a popular pastime for important Mycenaeans, and wild boar were a favorite prey. Other parts of the fresco show that hunters used chariots to chase the animals, while other men and women either rode in wagons or walked.

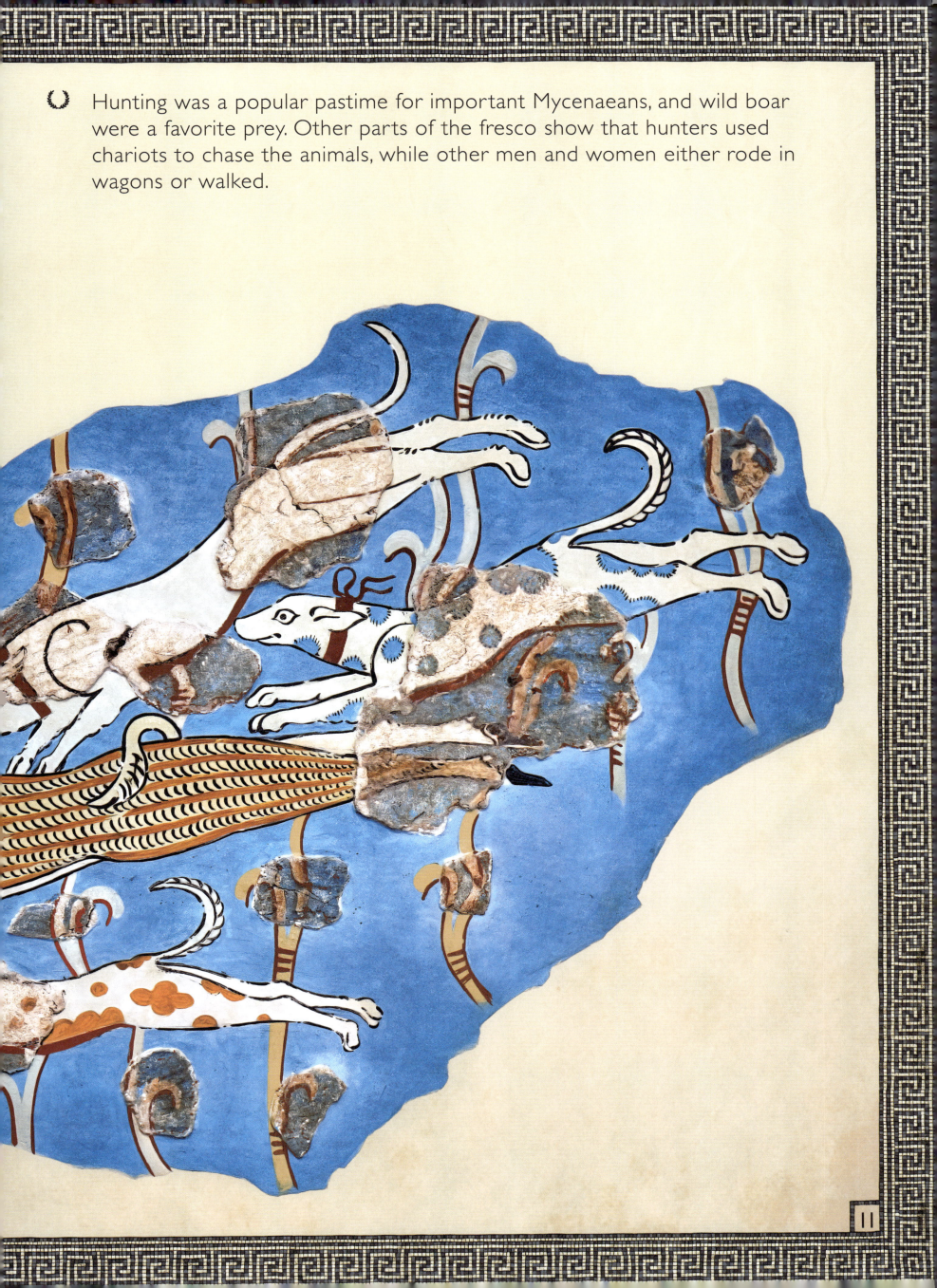

PERFUME BOTTLE

- This piece of ancient Greek pottery in the shape of a sandal hides a purpose. It once held perfume.

- Ancient Greek men and women used perfume in many parts of daily life. These included religious rituals as well as birth, marriage, and death ceremonies. They also used scents in aromatherapy in the hope they would improve their health and mood.

- The ancient Greeks often created humorous or quirky designs for their everyday objects. Other perfume bottles that have been discovered are shaped like a horse's head, a bird, a dolphin—and even the head of a hoplite soldier.

- The bottle is painted in the East Greek style. Artists from this area lived on Greek-speaking islands in the Aegean Sea and the west coast of modern-day Turkey, a region known as Ionia. The clay was pinker than that found on mainland Greece, and pottery was influenced by local art, especially in the use of floral and animal patterns.

- An ancient Greek philosopher named Theophrastus wrote an entire section of a book on perfumes and fragrances. "Concerning Odours" examined all the plants, oils, and spices that went into perfume ingredients, as well as a perfume's properties and medical uses.

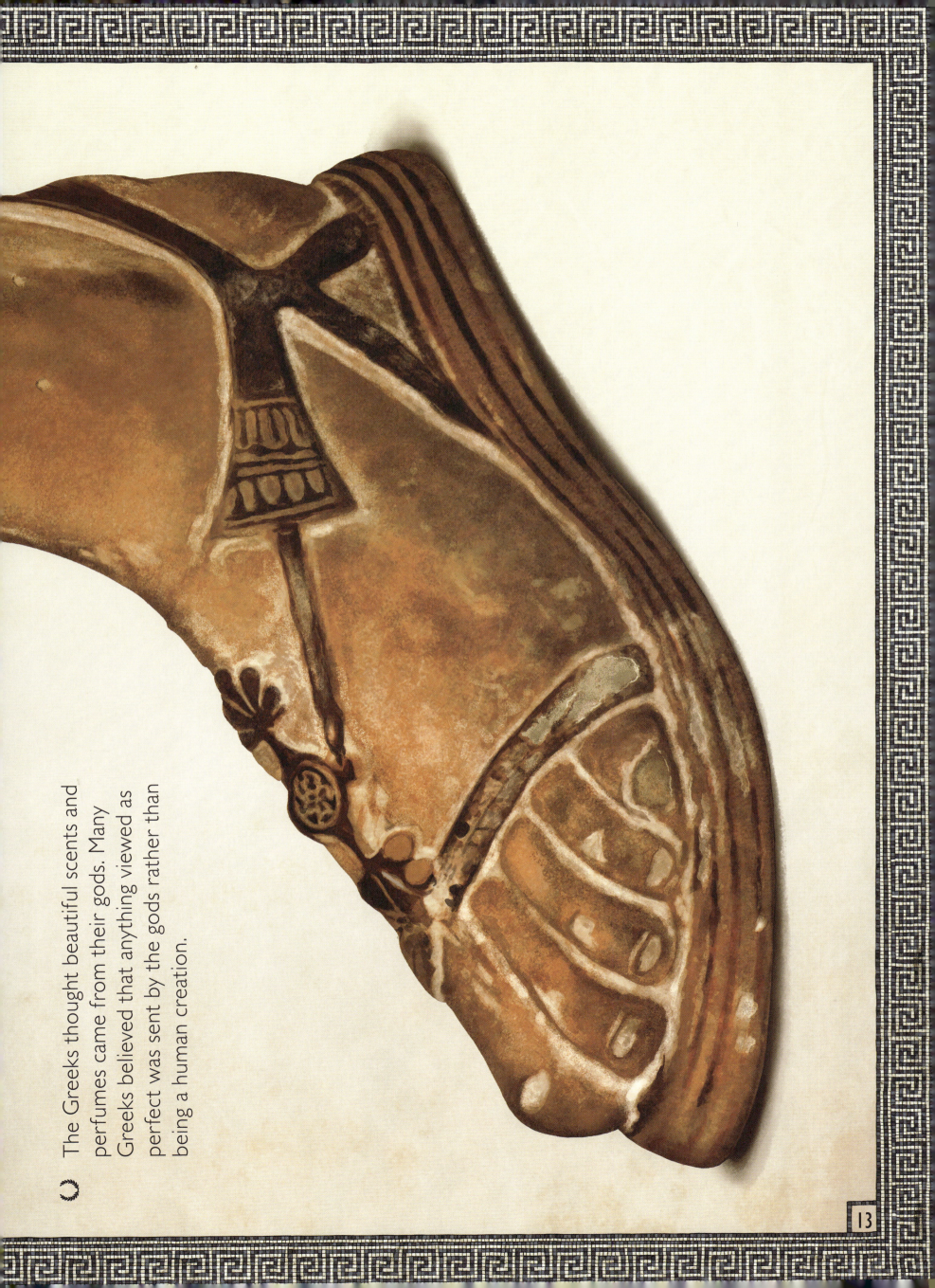

The Greeks thought beautiful scents and perfumes came from their gods. Many Greeks believed that anything viewed as perfect was sent by the gods rather than being a human creation.

A CHILD'S RATTLE

- This terra-cotta pig or wild boar is an ancient Greek rattle. When shaken, the rattle inside the animal's body makes a sound. We know from pictures on jugs and vases that ancient Greek babies played with rattles, just like they do today.

- This rattle was found in a grave. Some archaeologists believe this means it was the burial place of a baby or young child.

- As well as being a toy, the rattle might also have been designed to scare away evil spirits. The ancient Greeks believed in demons that could harm people, in life and in death.

- Rattles similar to this one have been found in the shrines of goddesses. They were probably placed there by women who hoped the goddess would help them to have a baby. In Athens, brides would donate their childhood toys to the goddess Artemis.

- The pig is made using Plain White Ware. This is a type of unpainted pottery found in ancient Cyprus, where the rattle was discovered.

- The rattle was created using a pottery wheel. The spinning wheel allowed the potter to shape the clay easily as it turned. The pig's mane was then pinched from the body and extra details carved into the animal before the clay was fired. The rattle was trapped inside.

- Nearly half of ancient Greek children did not live beyond the age of five. Children died from common diseases because the ancient Greeks did not have the medicines we use today. Parents hoped the rattle's sound would protect their child from any illnesses evil spirits might bring.

FACT FILE

Discovered: Salamis, Cyprus

Found today: British Museum, London, UK

Date: 300–50 BCE

Materials: Terra-cotta

Size: 4½ in (11.7 cm) long

PEBBLE MOSAIC

○ This large mosaic once covered the floor of a grand house in Eretria, an ancient city on the Greek island of Euboea.

○ Mosaics were made from lots of small, smooth pebbles or stones of different colors. They were carefully arranged to create patterns or mythological scenes. Later, colored glass, marble, or tile were also used.

○ The mosaic is packed with excitement. Lions attack horses on either side of a square. Above and below, female warriors fight griffins. These mythological beasts had the bodies, back legs, and tails of lions and the heads and wings of eagles.

○ The warriors on this mosaic are Arimaspians. In Greek mythology, the Arimaspians were a tribe of one-eyed people who tried to steal the gold of their neighbors, the griffins.

○ In a separate scene lower down, a Nereid, or female sea spirit, rides a sea monster called a hippocampus. This mythical creature was part horse and part fish or dolphin. The Nereid is Thetis, the mother of the hero Achilles. She is taking him his shield and spear.

○ Around the edge of the mosaic are geometric, or straight-sided, patterns. This was a popular design in ancient Greek art for centuries.

FACT FILE

Discovered: Eretria, Greece

Found today: House of the Mosaics, Eretria, Greece

Date: 370 BCE

Materials: Stone

Size: Main section 8 ft 9 in (2.65 m) long, 9 ft (2.8 m) wide; smaller section 3 ft (95 cm) long, 6 ft (1.8 m) wide

17

WINE CUP

- Larger than life, the god Dionysus lies back in comfort as he sails across the ocean. Dolphins swim around the ship and vines grow from its mast, ending in large bunches of grapes. The dolphins were pirates, who were changed into this form by Dionysus because they tried to rob him and throw him overboard.

- This beautiful cup is called a *kylix*. This type of cup was often used for drinking wine. The insides are usually decorated. As the drinker drained their *kylix*, pictures such as this one would be revealed.

- The *kylix* uses the pottery style known as black-figure. Designs were added to hard clay with a slip, or liquid clay, that turned black once the cup was fired. The background stayed the same red color. The black parts were then incised, or cut into, to create the details.

- The foot of the cup is signed by the master potter Exekias. He made some of the most impressive Greek vases known to us.

- A *kylix* was often used at a Greek symposium. This was a small party after a meal, where male guests could enjoy gossip, jokes, games, philosophy, and poetry. The cup's flat bottom was ideal for keeping wine from spilling as the men lay back on cushioned sofas.

FACT FILE

Discovered: Attica, Greece

Found today: State Collection of Antiquities, Munich, Germany

Date: 540–530 BCE

Materials: Terra-cotta

Size: 5¼ in (13.6 cm) high, 12 in (30.5 cm) wide

THE CHARIOT RACER

○ A young chariot racer calmly holds the horses' reins as he makes his victory lap around the hippodrome, or arena, after winning a race.

○ Chariot racing was one of ancient Greece's most popular sports. Spectators loved it for its speed, skill, and danger.

○ The chariot racer was the main piece in a larger group of statues erected around the Sanctuary of Apollo in Delphi. These included a two-wheeled chariot, at least four horses, and two grooms. Only fragments of the horses and chariot were found.

○ Very few bronze statues from ancient Greece still exist because the precious metal was often melted down years later to make other objects. This sculpture survived because it spent hundreds of years buried under a landslide.

○ The statue is in very good condition. Unusually for Greek bronzes, it still has its inlaid glass eyes. Only the youth's left arm, copper decoration on the lips and eyelashes, and the silver in his victory headband are missing.

- It is rare for males to be shown wearing clothes in ancient Greek art. This young man wears a *xystís*, or long tunic. A belt kept the *xystís* from billowing during the race.

- An inscription on the statue's base tells us it was set up by a Greek ruler in Sicily. He wanted to celebrate victories in the chariot races at Delphi's Pythian Games.

- The Pythian Games were one of ancient Greece's most important sporting competitions, held every four years. This statue was dedicated to the Greek god Apollo to give thanks for a win.

FACT FILE

Discovered: Sanctuary of Apollo, Delphi, Greece

Found today: Archaeological Museum of Delphi, Delphi, Greece

Date: 478–474 BCE

Materials: Bronze, silver, glass, colored stones

Size: 6 ft (1.8 m) high

MASK OF GOLD

○ This precious mask is made of glistening gold and was one of several discovered in a royal cemetery. It was once thought to show the face of a great king.

○ To make this mask, a sheet of gold was heated and hammered against a wooden mold. The details, such as the eyebrows, beard, and mustache, were then engraved into the metal using a sharp tool.

○ The mask was found in the ruins of the ancient city of Mycenae. This led some archaeologists to think the mask showed the legendary Greek king of Mycenae, Agamemnon. We now know it is even older than the time he was said to rule.

○ Mycenae was the center of a powerful Greek Bronze Age civilization known as the Mycenaean. The gold mask tells us that there was great wealth there. The Mycenaeans lived in walled hilltop cities, where daily life focused on a warrior king's palace at the heart of the settlement.

○ Objects like these are known as funerary masks. They covered the faces of important people in their graves and were a representation of what they looked like in life.

FACT FILE

Discovered: Mycenae, Greece

Found today: National Archaeological Museum, Athens, Greece

Date: 1550–1500 BCE

Materials: Gold

Size: About 12 in (30 cm) high

THE WARSHIP

○ Nine rowers heave on their oars as they row a warship across the sea. The ship on this piece of sculpted marble is a trireme. It was named after the three tiers of oars on each side that were used to row the ship. *Trireme* means "triple-oared" in ancient Greek.

○ This sculpture was dedicated on the Acropolis at Athens at a time when the Athenians were fighting the Spartans in the Peloponnesian War. This shows how much triremes were valued by the ancient Greeks.

○ Originally, this sculpture displayed twenty-five oarsmen. At the front stood an officer and at the back was a person who steered the ship. Warriors also stood on the deck.

○ Rowing a trireme all day was thirsty work. The ship carried with it nearly 2 gallons (8 liters) of water per rower to keep them hydrated each day.

○ A trireme's crew included about 170 rowers. They were citizens of the city that owned the ship, foreigners living in the city, and men from abroad.

FACT FILE

Discovered: Acropolis, Athens, Greece

Found today: Acropolis Museum, Athens, Greece

Date: 405 BCE

Materials: Marble

Size: 21¼ in (54 cm) wide, 15¾ in (40 cm) high

Triremes were made of soft, light wood to help them float. Ships were pulled from the sea at the end of a day's sailing to stop the wood absorbing too much water.

These boats were able to stay afloat even with a hole in the bottom. That is why no trireme shipwrecks have ever been found.

Space on a trireme was very limited. The people on board had to sleep on the beach their ship had been pulled onto each night.

ANCIENT COMPUTER

- This mechanism is one of the world's oldest examples of a computer. Its corroded metal masks an orrery—a machine used to predict the positions of the Sun, Moon, and planets.

- The clockwork device was found in a shipwreck off the coast of the Greek island of Antikythera in 1901. Alongside it were many other treasures, including magnificent bronze statues, precious jewelry, and a stunning coin hoard.

- The device was found as a single lump of bronze metal. Scientists were able to separate it into eighty-two fragments. This is the largest one.

- More than two thousand years ago, this complex instrument sat in a wooden box and contained more than thirty gears carrying thousands of tiny teeth. A hand crank pushed the gears around to power the mechanism.

- Small orbs for the stars and planets once moved around the mechanism's face, showing their position compared to Earth. A tiny model of the Moon rotated on a thin arm, flashing black and white to represent the real Moon's waxing and waning.

- The device was fitted with dials to record the days. One was even used to calculate the timing of the ancient Olympic Games!

FACT FILE

Discovered: Aegean Sea near Antikythera, Greece

Found today: National Archaeological Museum, Athens, Greece

Date: 205–60 BCE

Materials: Bronze

Size: Originally 13½ in (34 cm) high, 7 in (18 cm) wide, 3½ in (9 cm) deep; this piece is about 5 in (13 cm) wide

WARRIOR GODDESS

- The goddess Athena stands ready to fight, her arm raised to throw a spear, now missing, and holding what would have been a shield. On her head is a mighty helmet, with a crest in the shape of a swan's head.

- Draped across Athena's shoulders is her aegis, a cloak made of a monster's skin. It was used to terrify Athena's enemies and was all the more fearsome when it contained the hideous Gorgon Medusa's head in its center.

- This small statue was found near a temple decicated to Athena on the Acropolis in Athens. It has an inscription on its base, which tells us its origin—"Meleso dedicated it to Athena as a tithe." A tithe was a tribute in honor of a god or goddess.

- Athena was the patron goddess, or protector, of Athens. According to legend, she earned this honor by presenting the Athenians with an olive tree—something that could provide food, oil, shade, and wood. Her rival for the role, the sea god Poseidon, offered the city a spring, but it was of salt water and so could not be used for drinking or bathing.

- One of Athena's other names is Athena Promachos, or "Athena who fights on the front line." This is the name used when she is in the fighting form depicted in this statue.

FACT FILE

Discovered: Acropolis, Athens, Greece

Found today: Acropolis Museum, Athens, Greece

Date: 475–470 BCE

Materials: Bronze

Size: 12 in (30 cm) high

SCREECHING GRIFFINS

- A pair of bronze griffins open their mouths and curl their tongues to let out bloodcurdling screeches. In ancient Greek mythology, a griffin is a creature with the body of a lion and the head and wings of an eagle. Its front legs end in fearsome talons.

- The griffins are very well preserved. Even the eyes, which are inlaid with bone or ivory, are still partly intact.

- These griffins are protomes—decorations in the form of the front end of a human or animal. They were once fastened to a bronze cauldron.

- Griffins were thought to have protective powers. Perhaps the use of these ones as decorations on a cauldron was a way to keep such an expensive object safe.

- Ornate cauldrons like the one these griffins decorated were used as offerings to the gods. The cauldrons sat on stands or bases and were placed in temples and treasuries. The ancient Greeks hoped their expensive offerings would grant them favor with their chosen god.

- People worshipped many different gods in sacred spaces called sanctuaries. These places were inside a city or in the countryside. They contained a temple. Inside the temple was an image of the god, an altar, statues, and offerings to the god.

FACT FILE

Discovered: Samos, Greece

Found today: Art Institute of Chicago, Chicago

Date: 625–575 BCE

Materials: Bronze, bone or ivory

Size: 8–8½ in (20.3–21.6 cm) high, 3–3¼ in (7.6–8.3 cm) wide

31

WEDDING PROCESSION

- A decorated vase depicts the wedding of Peleus and Thetis. In Greek mythology, Peleus was a hero and the mortal king of Phthia, and Thetis was an immortal sea nymph.

- This type of vase is called a *dinos*. It was used to mix water and wine.

- A procession of guests approaches the married couple's home. In front of columns on the right stands the groom, Peleus. He welcomes, among others, the god Dionysus carrying a grapevine, the goddess Hebe in a white patterned dress, and, behind her, the half-horse, half-man Chiron.

- This vase's artist has used color to pick out different details. Red slip, or wet clay, is used for clothing and some animals. Traditional black is used for the males. White slip has been used to pick out female characters.

- Between the columns on the right are the words "Sophilos painted me" in ancient Greek. Sophilos was a very famous Greek painter.

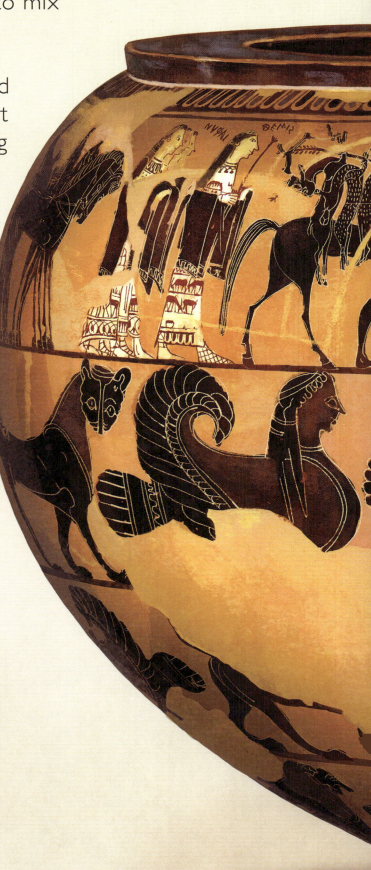

FACT FILE

Discovered: Attica, Greece

Found today: British Museum, London, UK

Date: 580–570 BCE

Materials: Terra-cotta

Size: 11¼ in (28.8 cm) high, 16½ in (42 cm) wide

In Greek mythology, Peleus and Thetis were the parents of Achilles, a great hero of the Trojan War. When the gods learned of a prophecy that the son of Thetis would be greater than his father, they decided that Thetis should marry Peleus. Because she was marrying a man and not a god, the gods hoped her child would not be powerful enough to threaten them.

SAYING GOODBYE

- A young girl gently holds her two pet doves. She quietly bids them farewell as she departs for her next life. This marble sculpture is a stele, or grave monument. It was set up by the girl's parents and represents their own goodbye to their dead child.

- Stelae in ancient Greece were used to mark graves. They were brightly painted and depicted a scene from the life of the deceased as a way to tell viewers something about that person. Markers for children often showed them with pets.

- The skilled carving of the girl's clothing and hair suggest her parents were wealthy enough to pay a talented artist. Poorer people also had grave markers built. These were not as grand—sometimes just a stone slab with a name inscribed.

- Many children born in ancient Greece did not survive childhood. The Greeks used a variety of burial practices for their children, which were sometimes different from how they buried adults. These included burying children in separate children's cemeteries.

- People were very rarely buried within a city because of disease and overcrowding in the areas where people lived. Grave markers were often clustered in burial grounds and along the roads outside of the city.

FACT FILE

Discovered: Paros, Greece

Found today: Metropolitan Museum of Art, New York City

Date: 450–440 BCE

Materials: Marble

Size: 31¾ in (80.6 cm) high

35

THE INCENSE BURNER

◡ This group of women sitting around a well was made as an object for burning incense. When lit, incense gives off a strong, perfumed smell.

◡ On each woman's head is a shallow bowl where incense was placed. The bowls, called calyxes, are shaped like flower stems.

◡ The women's bodies were all made from the same basic mold, but the arms and legs were added separately. This allowed the artist to vary their poses, creating a lively group of figures who almost seem to sway to music.

◡ The women hold several items—fruit, a bird, loaf of bread, fan, shallow bowl, or oil container. Some of these are symbols of the Greek goddesses Demeter and Persephone, so experts think this incense burner was used in their worship.

◡ The area of southern Italy this object is from was part of Magna Graecia, or Greater Greece. The region, which included Sicily, got this name due to its Greek-speaking inhabitants. These people had traveled from Greece and settled in Italy to set up colonies, or new communities. In time, they developed their own special culture.

FACT FILE

Discovered: Taranto (Taras), Italy

Found today: Metropolitan Museum of Art, New York City

Date: 300–350 BCE

Materials: Terra-cotta

Size: 8¼ in (21 cm) high

The incense burner is very well preserved, with yellow, red, and black paint that is still bright after more than two thousand years. The same colors are used for each figure but in different combinations to give the women their own personalities.

THE CALF BEARER

○ A bearded man effortlessly carries a calf on his shoulders. He is taking the animal to be sacrificed as an offering to the goddess Athena.

○ An inscription on the statue's base tells us that it was dedicated by Rhombos, son of Palos. The statue may be of Rhombos himself, a wealthy Athenian who could afford to place an expensive marble statue on the Acropolis.

○ This is an early type of Greek sculpture, inspired by Egyptian statues. Figures were upright and forward-facing, showing only simple details. The male figure in this style is called a *kouros* and the female is a *kore*.

○ The man's face shows very little emotion except for the slightly amused look given by his upturned lips. This expression is known as an archaic smile. It appears in many statues of this period.

○ Unlike the Egyptian statues they were based on, Greek sculptures usually showed men naked. This man wears a thin *himation*, or cloak, over his shoulders, but the rest of his body is unclothed. The *himation* was probably once painted to make it stand out.

The calf in the sculpture reminds us that the ancient Greeks depended on farming and raising animals to survive. Cows were not as common as other animals. Sheep and goats were the easiest livestock to rear, providing people with meat, wool, and milk for cheese.

Discovered: Acropolis, Athens, Greece

Found today: Acropolis Museum, Athens, Greece

Date: About 570 BCE

Materials: Marble, limestone

Size: 5 ft 5 in (1.65 m) high

SNAKE BRACELET

○ This ornate gold bracelet was one of a pair that once decorated the upper arms of a wealthy Greek woman. You can imagine her wearing them with pride as she welcomed important guests into her home.

○ The bracelet features two snakes, whose bodies are tied together to form a Heracles knot. The knot was an ancient symbol of love and marriage because it displayed a bond that could never be undone.

○ Snakes were a popular design for jewelry in ancient Greece. The two entwined snakes on this bracelet represent the hero Heracles's superhuman deed of killing two snakes while he was still in his cradle.

○ In myths, Heracles was the son of Zeus, the king of the gods, and Alcmene, a human. As a baby, Heracles used his great strength to kill a pair of snakes sent by the goddess Hera to harm him. Hera was the wife of Zeus, and she was jealous of Heracles's mother, Alcmene. The strong knot featured in this bracelet is named after Heracles.

○ The trend to wear bracelets in pairs copied Persian fashion of the time. From the mid-sixth century BCE, Greek cities in Ionia, an area of what is now Turkey, were under Persian rule.

FACT FILE

Discovered: Eretria, Greece

Found today: Pforzheim Jewelry Museum, Pforzheim, Germany

Date: 300–100 BCE

Materials: Gold, garnet

Size: 4½ in (11.5 cm) long

THEATER MASK

○ Theater was one of the most popular pastimes in ancient Greece and drew audiences from all levels of society—even prisoners. This terra-cotta mask of a young satyr is a smaller model of one worn onstage by ancient Greek actors.

○ In ancient Greek mythology, satyrs are wild half-man, half-goat embodiments of nature. They have animal-like features and live in the woods. This is symbolized in the mask by wide staring eyes, pointed ears, and an ivy wreath crown.

○ All actors in ancient Greek theater were male. Masks allowed actors to play various roles, including women. Different masks told the audience the character's age, gender, and level of importance, or if they had changed their appearance.

○ The character this mask portrays appeared in a comedic play. Comedy was one of the three types of Greek theater, alongside tragedy and satyr plays. The satyr play was related to both tragedy and comedy.

○ Theater spread across the Greek world from Athens. Many cities built open-air theaters as key parts of their public spaces. They were shaped as semicircles and were built into hillsides, which provided natural seating areas and meant that everyone could see and hear well.

FACT FILE

Discovered: Sicily, Italy

Found today: Getty Villa Museum, Malibu, CA

Date: 200–100 BCE

Materials: Terra-cotta

Size: 4¾ in (12 cm) high, 6 in (15.5 cm) wide

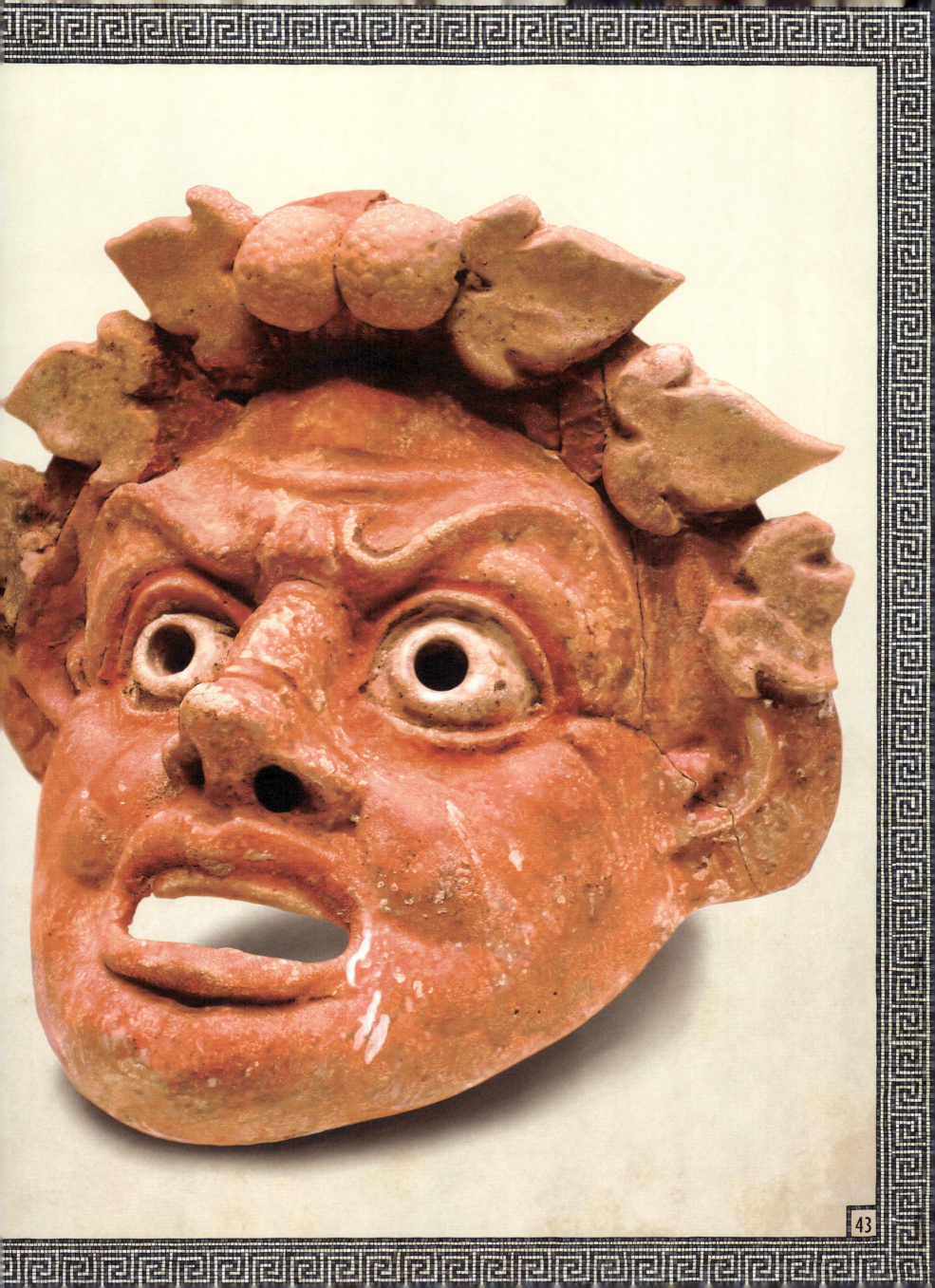

43

A SOLDIER'S CUIRASS

- The bronze cuirass, or breastplate, was an important part of an ancient Greek soldier's panoply—their complete suit of armor. The front part shown here was fastened to a backplate so that the whole torso was protected from sword and spear blows.

- Ancient Greek foot soldiers were known as hoplites. Armed with spears and shields, they made up the main part of Greek armies. Hoplites successfully defended Greece when the Persian Empire twice tried to conquer it.

- This cuirass has been designed to look like the body of a man. This made the wearer look more heroic to the Greeks, who prized the perfect male torso. Such an athletic appearance might also have helped intimidate enemies on the battlefield.

- This type of breastplate is called a bell cuirass because it is wider at the bottom, like a bell. It gave soldiers greater movement at the hips, allowing them to bend over more easily.

- Soldiers also used lighter body armor called *linothorax*, which was made from strengthened linen. This was cheaper, cooler, and lighter than the heavier metal cuirasses, which were sometimes difficult to fight in.

FACT FILE

Discovered: Apulia, Italy

Found today: Metropolitan Museum of Art, New York City

Date: 400–300 BCE

Materials: Bronze

Size: 19½ in (49.8 cm) high

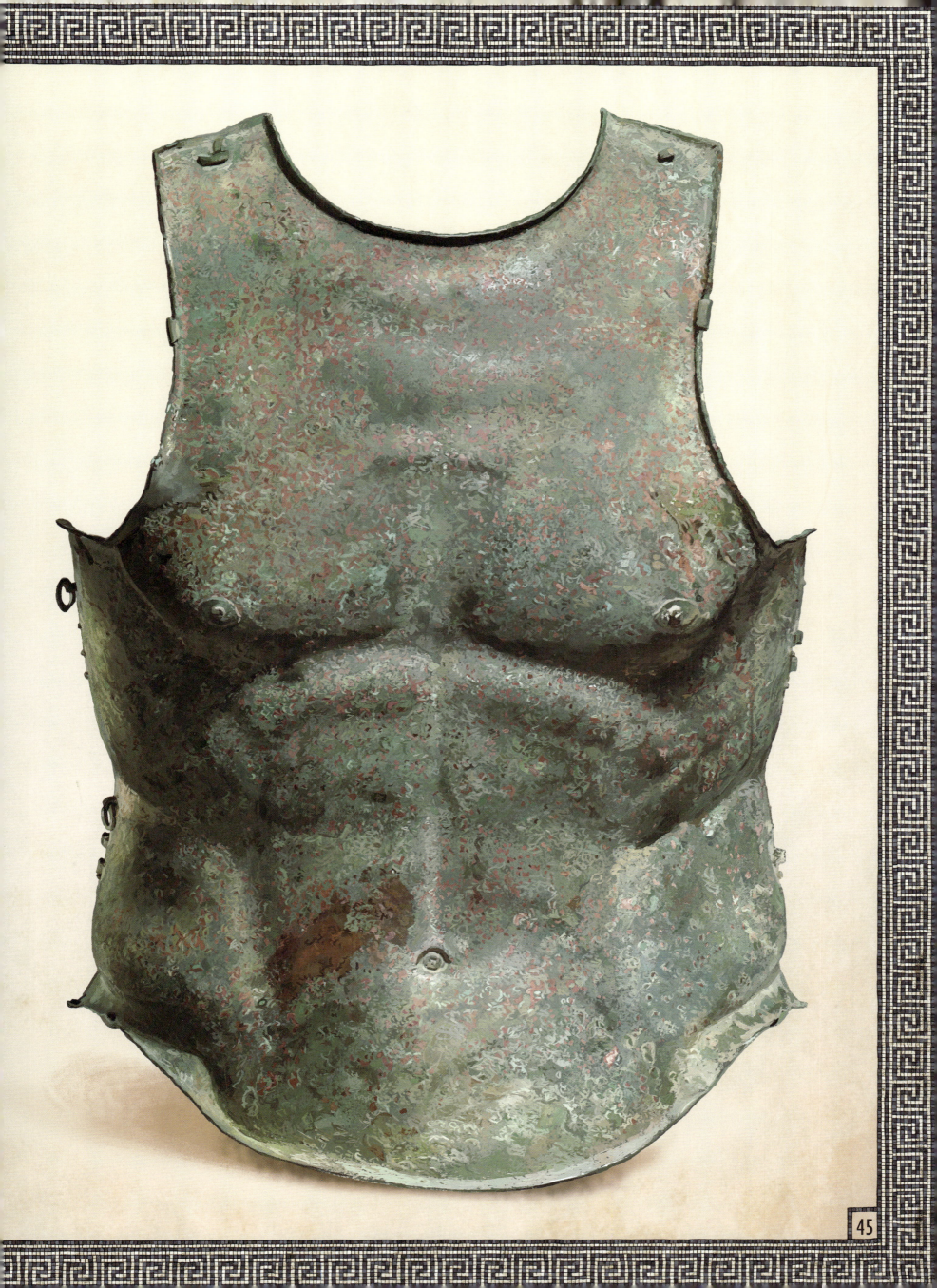

THE TOY HORSE

⚜ Ancient Greek children enjoyed playing with toys, such as this little horse on wheels. It is easy to imagine cries of delight as it was pulled over bumpy ground.

⚜ The toy horse has a hole in its nose. A piece of string was threaded through the hole so that it could be pulled along.

⚜ The features on the toy are simple. A series of triangles, one inside the other, decorates the front of the horse's neck. The body is painted with black slip, or liquid clay, and the mane and tail are striped.

⚜ This toy was found in a grave that is nearly three thousand years old. Perhaps it was placed there to be used in the afterlife or as an offering to the gods. The grave was outside the city walls of Athens, in an area called the Kerameikos. It was once the potters' quarter.

⚜ The ancient Greeks believed play was important for children. The great philosopher Plato even wrote that parents should encourage it.

FACT FILE

Discovered: Athens, Greece

Found today: Archaeological Museum of Kerameikos, Athens, Greece

Date: 950–900 BCE

Materials: Terra-cotta

Size: 3¾ in (9.3 cm) high

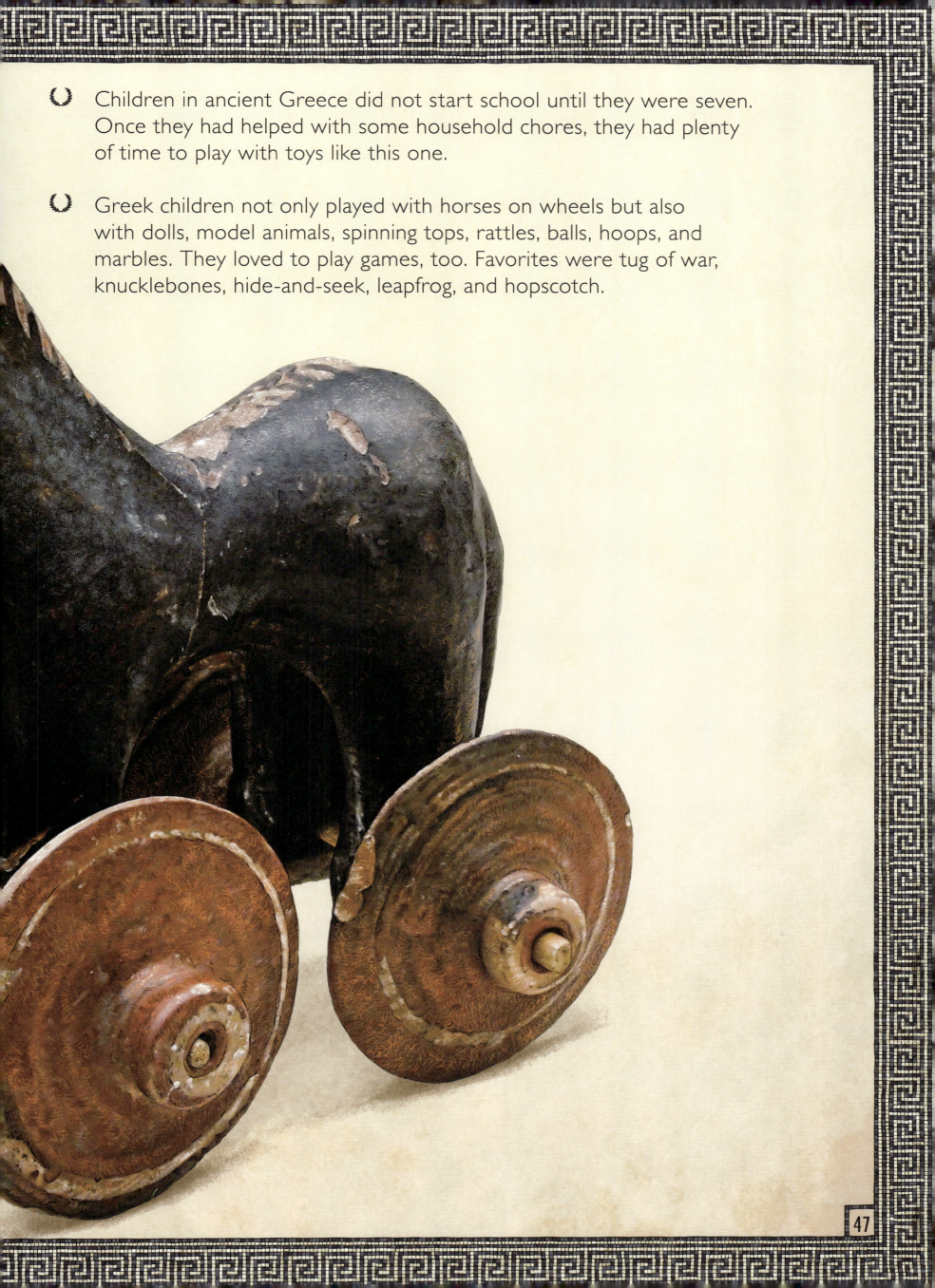

○ Children in ancient Greece did not start school until they were seven. Once they had helped with some household chores, they had plenty of time to play with toys like this one.

○ Greek children not only played with horses on wheels but also with dolls, model animals, spinning tops, rattles, balls, hoops, and marbles. They loved to play games, too. Favorites were tug of war, knucklebones, hide-and-seek, leapfrog, and hopscotch.

FACE OF A CONQUEROR

○ This shining silver coin shows the face of Alexander the Great, a king of Macedon in northern Greece and a mighty conqueror. It is a tetradrachm, worth four times a man's average daily wage.

○ Alexander became king when he was twenty years old. In a little over ten years, he conquered most of the Greek world, Egypt, and the Persian Empire and even led his armies into India.

○ This coin was minted, or made, by Alexander's former general Lysimachus. We know this because of an inscription on the other side of the coin that reads, "Of King Lysimachus."

○ After Alexander died, his empire was divided between his generals. Lysimachus took Thrace in northern Greece and, later, parts of what is now Turkey. He used Alexander's face on his coins to show people that he was the former king's true heir.

○ The coin shows Alexander with the ram's horns of the Egyptian god Amun. This was intended to link the two in the minds of the people, telling them that the deceased Alexander was now a god.

FACT FILE

Discovered: Lampsacus, Turkey

Found today: British Museum, London, UK

Date: 305–281 BCE

Materials: Silver

Weight: ½ oz (17.25 g)

DISCUS THROWER

○ This statue of a young man preparing to throw a discus perfectly captures the moment between his backswing and the discus's release. It is one of the most famous pieces of ancient Greek art.

○ The marble sculpture is a Roman copy of an earlier Greek statue, which is now lost. The original was made by the master sculptor Myron using bronze. So many copies of it were made that experts can be sure of how it once looked.

○ Myron's statue gives a striking impression of an athlete in the middle of movement, but it is not really how the body would look during such a strenuous action. Artists at this time wanted to show a perfect human body, so the face remains calm, and the muscles are not strained by the athlete's movement.

○ The discus throw was one of the sports at the ancient Olympic Games. It was performed as part of the pentathlon, which featured five different events. Athletes would compete naked, and the winners would be crowned with an olive-leaf wreath.

○ The ancient Olympic Games were held at the religious sanctuary of Olympia in honor of the Greek god Zeus. The cities that sent athletes to the games were often at war with one another. A period of peace was announced during the games so that everyone could travel to Olympia safely.

FACT FILE

Discovered: Rome, Italy (this copy)

Found today: National Rome Museum, Rome

Date: 460–450 BCE (original); about 150 BCE (this copy)

Materials: Marble (originally bronze)

Size: 5 ft 1 in (1.55 m) high

MUSIC OF THE SIRENS

○ A ship sails past the island of the Sirens. These strange creatures—half woman, half bird—sing their irresistible song to tempt the sailors to jump into the sea to reach them. The hero Odysseus is strapped to the mast. He has told his men to plug their ears and not to untie him until they have passed, so that he alone could hear the beautiful music without being lured to his death.

○ The scene on this vase is a famous episode from Greek mythology. It depicts one of the stories from Odysseus's ten-year journey home to Ithaca after the end of the Trojan War.

○ This type of vase is a *stamnos*. It was used to store liquids. Artists decorated their finer pottery with mythological scenes. Today, we can use this pottery to learn about the ancient Greeks' culture and beliefs.

○ The *stamnos* is decorated in the pottery style known as red-figure. A pot's background was coated with a slip, or liquid clay, which turned black when the cup was fired. Everything else remained the red of the pot.

○ The story shown on this vase was also told by the poet Homer in his epic poem *The Odyssey*, written more than twenty-five hundred years ago. Homer collected many stories of heroic deeds that had been recited by the ancient Greeks for generations.

FACT FILE

Discovered: Vulci, Italy

Found today: British Museum, London, UK

Date: 480–470 BCE

Materials: Terra-cotta

Size: 13½ in (34 cm) high, 15 in (38 cm) wide

BRONZE MIRROR

- This circular bronze mirror belonged to a wealthy ancient Greek woman. It was once polished so brightly that its owner could see her reflection in it. Over time, it has lost its shine and changed color.

- Bronze mirrors have a long history going back nearly five thousand years. The early Greek Minoan and Mycenaean civilizations were the first to use them in Europe, but they have also been found across the world, from Egypt and West Asia to China.

- Mirrors are often associated with women in ancient Greek culture. They have been found in women's graves and as dedications to goddesses in sanctuaries. Even the mirrors themselves display women, like this one does.

- This mirror was not meant to be held but to stand on its own. In place of a handle is a woman wearing a *peplos*, an ancient Greek dress. This design is known as a caryatid mirror. Caryatids are pillars or columns shaped as female figures.

- Two winged children known as Erotes fly above the woman's head. These mythological figures represented love. A sphinx or Siren would once have sat on the top of the disc. Around the edge were dogs chasing hares—now just the two hares remain. Taken together, these symbolize the pursuit of love.

- The ancient Greeks believed mirrors had magical properties. They thought mirrors were windows into the future, bringing knowledge and prophecy. But the Greeks also feared mirrors. They believed if a person gazed into a mirror too long, their soul could be stolen.

- The power of reflections is shown in the Greek myth of Narcissus, a beautiful man who rejected all his admirers. One day, Narcissus caught sight of his reflection in a pool. He fell deeply in love with his own image, but upon realizing his feelings could not be returned, he wasted away.

HORSE OF SELENE

○ This horse's head is one of the sculptures from the Parthenon on the Acropolis of Athens, the grandest and most famous of all ancient Greek temples. The building was dedicated to the goddess Athena, whom the city was named after.

○ The head was located in the Parthenon's east pediment. A pediment is the triangular space at the end of a building, just under the pointed roof. In Greek temples, these spaces were usually filled with sculptures that told a story from mythology.

○ This statue represents one of the horses that drew the chariot of the moon goddess Selene. The horse is shown straining as it pulls. Its ears are flattened, its jaw is open, its nostrils flare, and its eyes bulge. Small holes show where a bridle was once attached.

○ The lifelike details on the horse show us how advanced ancient Greek sculpture became. This and other statues decorating the Parthenon were created by Pheidias, one of the greatest sculptors of the ancient world.

○ The horse's head fit into one corner of a scene that told the story of the goddess Athena's miraculous birth. Athena sprang from her father Zeus's head fully grown, armed and dressed for battle.

○ The Parthenon's pediments were once filled by fifty colossal sculptures. Over the centuries, many have been lost, damaged, or removed. The horse's head is one of the few surviving pieces, and one of the best preserved.

PROCESSION TO A SACRIFICE

⟨ ⟩ This painted piece of wood is the oldest known example of ancient Greek panel painting. It is one of a set of four that were discovered nearly one hundred years ago in a deep cave in Greece.

⟨ ⟩ A religious scene depicts a young boy leading a lamb to sacrifice. Behind him are two other boys playing musical instruments and two women. At the end of the procession, barely visible now, is a bearded man. The woman at the altar on the right carries a tray of items on her head and is pouring liquid from a jug as a libation, or religious offering.

○ The panel is probably a dedication to nature spirits called nymphs. Wealthy people made offerings to the gods using expensive materials like marble and bronze. This simple wooden panel was likely to have been offered by a less well-off person or family.

○ The unusual conditions in the cave in which the panels were found stopped the wood from rotting and kept the brightness of the colored paints for 2,500 years. Wood does not usually preserve well, which is why this surviving piece is so important in helping us understand ancient Greek panel painting.

○ The two instruments being played are an *aulos*, or double flute, and a lyre. Music was played alongside the recital of poetry and at weddings, funerals, and plays. The lyre was also the chosen instrument of the famous mythological musician Orpheus and the god Apollo.

FACT FILE

Discovered: Pitsa, Corinthia, Greece

Found today: National Archaeological Museum, Athens, Greece

Date: 540–530 BCE

Materials: Wood, plaster, paint

Size: 6 in (15 cm) high, 12¾ in (32.3 cm) long

MEDUSA'S STARE

- With her huge eyes, sharp tusks, lolling tongue, and snakes curling at her neck, Medusa is a terrifying sight. In Greek mythology, Medusa is one of the three Gorgons, monstrous sisters who could turn anyone looking at them to stone.

- This sculpture is an antefix, or ancient roof ornament. Placed upright along a building's outer edges, antefixes protected the ends of the last row of roof tiles. Gorgon heads were a popular design because people believed they would scare evil away from the building.

- The black, red, and ocher paint on the antefix is very well-preserved. The colors are used to highlight the Gorgon's terrible features.

- Medusa was once beautiful. The myth tells how she angered the goddess Athena, who turned her into a hideous monster with living snakes for hair.

- The Greek hero Perseus was sent to kill Medusa. He used a shiny shield to look at Medusa's reflection instead of into her eyes, which would have turned him to stone. With his sharp sword, he sliced off her head and gave it to Athena as a trophy.

FACT FILE

Discovered: Acropolis, Athens, Greece

Found today: Acropolis Museum, Athens, Greece

Date: About 510–500 BCE

Materials: Terra-cotta

Size: 7¾ in (19.5 cm) high, 8 in (20 cm) wide

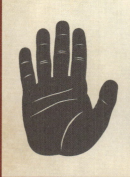

Medusa's face was often depicted on soldiers' shields to strike fear into the hearts of their enemies. It was also put on the doors of ovens to remind people not to open them too soon.

THE GRANARY CHEST

◌ This patterned chest was found in the grave of a wealthy woman from Athens. On its lid are models of five granaries—containers for storing cereal grains.

◌ The decorations on the rounded granaries and the chest are in the Geometric style. This style used a series of simple repeating patterns and borders. The continuous snaking line is called a meander.

◌ Buried alongside this chest were around eighty other objects, including gold rings and earrings and a necklace of glass beads. It is the richest grave ever found from this period.

FACT FILE

Discovered: The Areopagus, Athens, Greece

Found today: Ancient Agora Museum, Athens, Greece

Date: About 850 BCE

Materials: Clay

Size: 17½ in (44.5 cm) long, 10 in (25 cm) high, 3¾ in (9.5 cm) deep

Funerals for wealthy ancient Greeks were lavish and sometimes included a large feast. People were buried with precious possessions and models of things that had been a significant part of their lives.

This chest's burial in a grave tells us that granaries and the grain they held were important to the deceased woman. They represent the wealth she had enjoyed from farming.

The model granary chest is a reminder that grain was the most important food source in ancient Greece. Olives and grapes were also central to Greek culture.

JOINTED DOLL

○ Many toys that children enjoy playing with today had versions used in ancient Greece. This *plagon*, or painted doll, would have been owned by a young girl.

○ Women in ancient Greece had strict roles in society, including raising children. It is thought that caring for dolls helped young girls to prepare for adulthood.

○ The limbs of the doll are joined to the body using thread. This allowed them to be moved.

○ Many *plaggona* have been found in tombs and sanctuaries. This tells us they were originally religious figurines and were perhaps used in household worship. They later came to be used as dolls.

○ This *plagon* wears a short tunic and a cylinder-shaped headdress on top of her dark hair. Similar dolls to this one also had shoes.

○ The doll's clothing might mean it represents a type of dancer who dressed this way. Some of the jointed dolls that have been discovered carry cymbals or castanets.

- Unpainted dolls might have been dressed in clothes sewn from rags by the girls or the women of the house.

- Dolls held an important role even when girls grew older. *Plaggona* were dedicated to the goddess Artemis on the day before a girl's wedding. In Greek belief, Artemis helped women prepare for childbirth.

- Some experts think the *plaggona* are too fragile to be real dolls. Perhaps they were hung up as charms, with their swaying movement designed to keep away evil spirits.

FACT FILE

Discovered: Probably Corinth, Greece

Found today: Metropolitan Museum of Art, New York City

Date: 500–400 BCE

Materials: Terra-cotta

Size: 4¾ in (12 cm) high

BLADE OF A KING

○ Golden wild cats race between papyrus plants as they chase ducks through the shallows, and fish jump out of the water in fright. The action-packed scene decorates a bronze blade that would once have been polished until it shone.

○ This type of blade was part of a short sword or dagger. These were used by ancient Greek warriors alongside a spear or javelin.

○ The blade was found in the city of Mycenae's royal cemetery. The grave this object was placed in contained three males. Buried with them was a wealth of treasures. These included golden death masks, gold and bronze armor and weapons, and an ostrich-egg drinking cup.

○ This blade was forged in the Mycenaean Greek period more than three thousand years ago. This time in world history is known as the Bronze Age because metal objects were made of bronze rather than iron or steel.

Scenes like the one on the blade are called Nilotic because they depict plants and animals from the River Nile in Egypt. Mycenaean Greece and Egypt had strong trade and cultural connections.

Such an ornate dagger was probably not intended to be used in war. Only a person of very high rank, such as a king, could have afforded one.

FACT FILE

Discovered: Mycenae, Greece

Found today: National Archaeological Museum, Athens, Greece

Date: 1600–1500 BCE

Materials: Bronze, gold, silver

Size: 6½ in (16.3 cm) long, 2 in (4.7 cm) wide

THE EAGLE CUP

○ This characterful one-handled cup is a *rhyton*. These cups were used for drinking liquids or pouring libations. These were religious acts that required fluids to be poured as part of an offering to a god.

○ The *rhyton* is in the shape of a fearsome eagle. On its beak are a series of score marks. *Rhyta* were often used outside, and the marks helped to give a better grip when the cup was stuck into the earth between sips.

○ Some *rhyta* had a small hole at the bottom. The hole was covered with a thumb while the *rhyton* was filled at the wide opening. The drinker would then release their thumb and tip their head back to let the liquid pour into their mouth. Other types of *rhyton* were used as normal drinking cups.

○ *Rhyta* were used for many centuries before this one was made in ancient Greece. They have been found in remains from ancient Persia—modern-day Iran—through to the Minoan civilization on Crete.

○ In ancient Greek mythology, the eagle was a symbol of Zeus, the king of the gods. Eagles were thought to be Zeus's messengers and heralds of victory, and to have the ability to see the future. These connections led later leaders, from Alexander the Great to Roman emperors, to use eagles as their own symbols.

○ Lots of different kinds of *rhyton* have been found. Many feature the heads of animals such as rams, horses, and dogs.

FACT FILE

Discovered: Capua, Italy

Found today: British Museum, London, UK

Date: 500–470 BCE

Materials: Terra-cotta

Size: 9½ in (24.1 cm) high, 5 in (12.7 cm) wide

THE VICIOUS SPHINX

◖◗ This stunning marble sphinx once marked the grave of a youth and a little girl. In Greek mythology, a sphinx is a fearsome creature with the head and chest of a woman, body of a lion, wings of an eagle, and a tail in the form of a snake.

◖◗ The sphinx sat on top of a tall column that was carved with images of the young people buried there. They must have come from a wealthy family to have had such an elaborate grave monument.

◖◗ The ancient Greeks decorated some of their grave monuments with sphinxes in the hope that the creature would scare away grave robbers.

◖◗ Ancient Greek sculptures were not the color of the marble they were carved from. This sphinx has traces of red, black, and blue paint, which tells us that the Greeks painted their statues. The colors have faded or flaked off over the centuries.

◖◗ The sphinx plays a big role in the story of a mythical Greek king named Oedipus. In the tale, the sphinx devours travelers near the city of Thebes unless they can answer her impossible riddle. Oedipus defeated the sphinx by answering correctly. In a rage, she threw herself from her mountain lair and died, ridding the city of her menace.

FACT FILE

Discovered: Kataphygi, Attica, Greece

Found today: Metropolitan Museum of Art, New York City

Date: About 530 BCE

Materials: Marble

Size: 4 ft 8¼ in (1.43 m) high, including column capital (not shown)

THE HORSE RACER

- A young boy braces himself against a horse as it springs through the air. This is one of the few bronze sculptures to survive from ancient Greece.

- Most ancient Greek bronze sculptures were melted down for their valuable metal long ago. This one still exists because it was lost on an ancient shipwreck. When the wreck was discovered, the horse and rider were found lying among countless other treasures.

- Horses were used for warfare, racing, traveling, and hunting. They were a popular subject in ancient Greek art.

- An image of Nike, the goddess of victory, is engraved on the horse's right thigh. This tells us it is a racing horse.

- The sculpture is life-size and very realistic. It is well-preserved, although the rider's whip and the horse's reins and bridle are missing.

- The young rider shows off his skill as he clings to the horse's back. Experts think the boy is from Africa, while his hairstyle hints he might also have Greek family.

FACT FILE

Discovered: Aegean Sea near Cape Artemision, Euboea, Greece

Found today: National Archaeological Museum, Athens, Greece

Date: 150–140 BCE

Materials: Bronze

Size: 6 ft 10¾ in (2.1 m) high, 9 ft 6¼ in (2.9 m) long

The large and impressive sculpture is thought to have been dedicated to the gods by a wealthy Greek who wanted to give thanks for horse-racing victories. This suggests how important sports, competition, and prestige were in ancient Greece.

FIERCE CENTAUR

This relief, or shallow sculpture, depicts a centaur about to attack a panther. The centaur's face appears calm, not giving away his violent intentions as he raises his club.

Centaurs were mythological creatures that were part horse, part human. In the stories told about them, they are wild and cannot be tamed. Female centaurs are called centaurides.

This relief panel is from a sarcophagus, a type of carved coffin. Only the wealthiest Greeks could afford to be buried in a sarcophagus with sculpted decoration like this.

The most famous centaur in Greek mythology was Chiron. Unlike most centaurs, he was well-educated and known for training some of Greece's mightiest heroes, such as Jason and Achilles.

In ancient Greek art, centaurs are often shown fighting a tribe of people called the Lapiths. The myth describes how the centaurs tried to carry off the Lapith women. The hero Theseus and the Lapiths fought with the centaurs and drove them off.

On the other side of this panel are the remains of another sculpture that once showed the goddess Athena and two worshippers. Perhaps the centaur artist used the back of the earlier Athena design, which might never have been finished.

FACT FILE

Discovered: Rome, Italy

Found today: World Museum, Liverpool, UK

Date: 500–300 BCE

Materials: Marble

Size: 16 in (41 cm) high, 13½ in (34.5 cm) wide

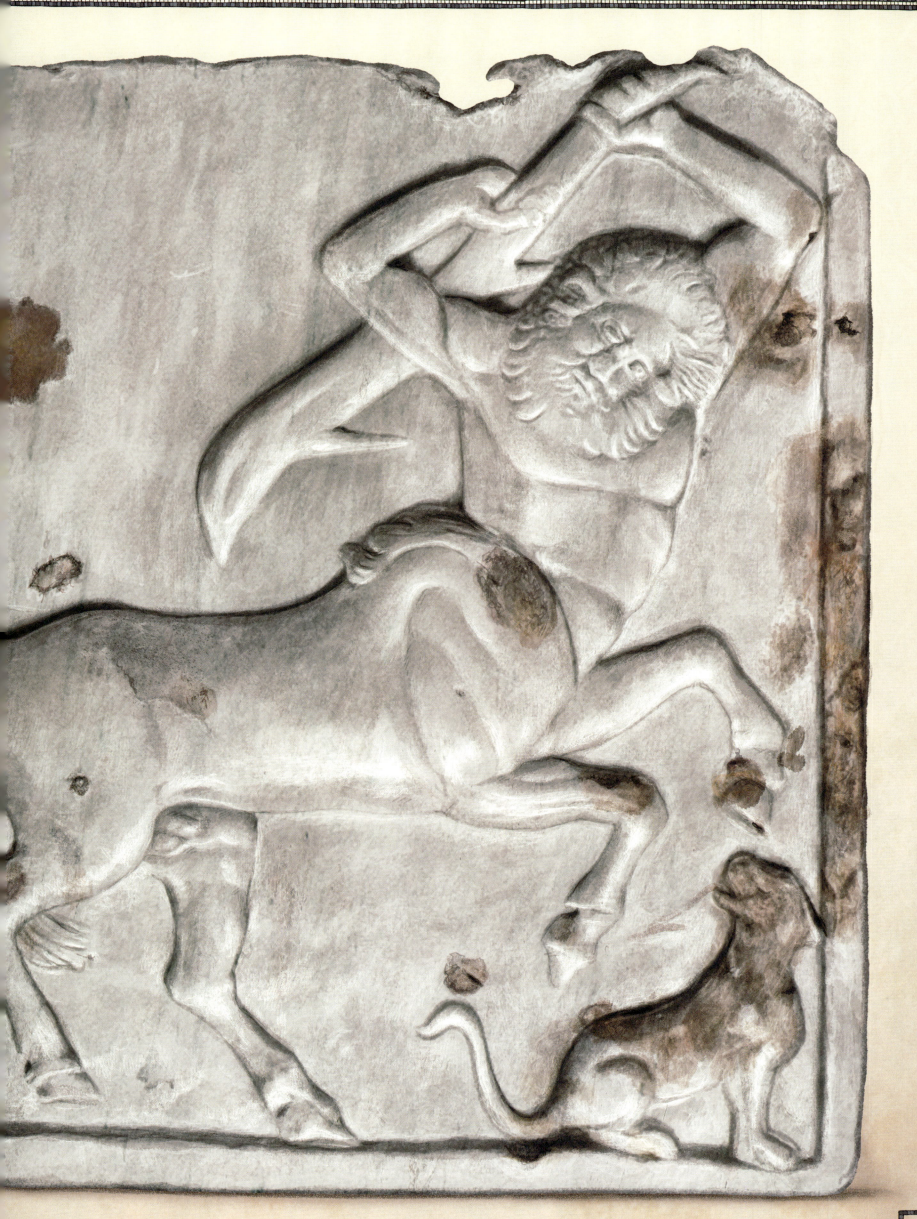

THE LITTLE OWL

○ This little owl is an *aryballos*, a flask used to hold olive oil or perfume. The liquid could be poured out of an opening in the bird's tail.

○ On the base of the *aryballos* is a hole. A lace was threaded through the hole so the flask could be easily carried. Ancient Greek art often shows *aryballoi* strapped to athletes' wrists or hung on pegs at the bathhouse.

○ Even though the flask was a practical object rather than an ornament, the artist has taken care over its decoration. Red and black paint are used on the owl's beak and feathers, bringing the little bird to life.

○ Olive oil was very important in ancient Greek culture. Together with the olive tree's fruit, it was the basis of Greek cooking. Oil was combined with perfume and worn on special occasions. It was also used as fuel for lamps as well as in medicine and religious ceremonies.

○ In ancient Greece, owls were associated with Athena, the goddess of wisdom and protector of Athens. To celebrate her, the people of Athens put the goddess's bird on their silver coins. In time, the coins themselves came to be called *glaukes*, or owls.

FACT FILE

Discovered: Corinth, Greece

Found today: State Collection of Antiquities, Munich, Germany

Date: About 630 BCE

Materials: Terra-cotta

Size: 2¼ in (5.6 cm) high, 1½ in (3.6 cm) wide, 2¼ in (6 cm) deep

THE WINGED VICTORY

○ The wind whips at the robes of Nike as she descends to the deck of a ship. Nike is the winged ancient Greek goddess of victory.

○ The statue has an additional part—a sculpted base in the shape of a warship's bow, the front end of a ship. Nike is placed on this base as if she is landing from the sky. Her clothes are blown by the strong wind. Perhaps she has come to help the ship's sailors, who are struggling in a storm.

○ Many parts of the original Nike are missing. These include the head, both arms—one of which was raised—both feet, and the right wing. The right wing that can be seen on the statue today is a plaster copy of the left wing in mirror image.

○ This sculpture was considered a masterpiece in the time it was made. It was even shown on silver coins of the era. This gives us a good idea of how it originally looked.

○ The Nike was made in the Hellenistic period of ancient Greece. Art from this time celebrates the expansion of Greek culture after the death of the conqueror king Alexander the Great in 323 BCE. Sculptures often show powerful themes and strong emotions in a very realistic way.

○ The Nike and other sculptures were removed from Greece many years ago. The Greek government is now asking museums around the world to return these priceless artworks, which represent important parts of Greek culture and history.

FACT FILE

Discovered: Samothrace, Greece

Found today: Louvre Museum, Paris, France

Date: 200–175 BCE

Materials: Marble

Size: 10 ft 9 in (3.28 m) high

ANCIENT GREECE

ASIA MINOR

IONIA

AEGEAN SEA

ATTICA

Athens

Mycenae

Sparta

Olympia

AFRICA

MEDITERRANEAN SEA

Athens

Attica

N
E
S
W